LADY OF COURAGE

THE STORY OF LOTTIE MOON

by Ann Kilner Hughes

Dedication

This book is dedicated to my parents, whose lives were my earliest evidence of the gospel.

Acknowledgements

My thanks to Catherine B. Allen, author of *The New Lottie Moon Story*, and my special thanks to my husband, David, for his encouragement in the writing of this book.

Published by Woman's Missionary Union, SBC
P. O. Box 830010
Birmingham, AL 35283-0010

Design by Telicia Montague and Kelly Vornauf

ISBN: 1-56309-159-3
W877110•0101•2M5

Table of Contents

1

Growing Up at Viewmont

The October sun gave a golden glow to the ripe apples on the trees in the Moon family orchard. The leaves rustled in the gentle wind. One by one the leaves turned loose and drifted to the ground. An occasional apple fell with a *kerplunk* that broke the afternoon quiet.

Lottie Moon was busily picking plump, ripe apples. The cook had promised to bake apple pies tomorrow. Lottie loved the outdoors on beautiful days like this. She also loved the sweet-tart taste of hot apple pie.

"Lottie, Lottie, where are you? Mother says we have to dress for dinner now!" Orianna Moon called across the yard and into the orchard.

Lottie's eyes danced with mischief when she heard her older sister calling her. She slipped behind a tree and did not make a sound.

Orianna came closer to the orchard. She began to scold Lottie in her big sister way.

"You know there's a visiting preacher coming for dinner, and Mama says we'd better be on time," she said.

Just when Orianna reached the spot where Lottie was hiding, the younger girl popped from behind the tree, grabbed her basket of apples, and ran toward the kitchen. A surprised Orianna followed close behind.

"Make sure you're not late!" Lottie called back over her shoulder as Orianna hurried to catch up.

Lottie did not like having to leave the freedom of the apple orchard just to go inside and get dressed up. But she liked having company for dinner. When company came, the cook loaded the table with homemade biscuits, ham, chicken and gravy, and fresh vegetables. Guests often told exciting stories about faraway places. Lottie liked to hear their stories. She liked to ask questions about the people and places they had seen. Often she had more questions than her mother allowed her to ask. In proper households of that time, children were expected to sit quietly and listen to adult conversation unless someone spoke to them.

The Moon household was very proper. Often, while the adults were talking, Lottie used her imagination to fill in the details of their stories. Sometimes she imagined herself in the faraway places they described.

Lottie's full name was Charlotte Digges Moon. She was happy living with her family on Viewmont, their large farm in Albemarle County, Virginia. But she was very curious about the world beyond her home. Her bright mind was always full of questions.

Lottie had many opportunities to learn, for her parents believed strongly in education for both boys and girls. Mrs. Moon brought the best tutors available to live in their home. The tutors taught the Moon children reading, grammar, music, and French. The tutors taught the children until the children went away to high school. Mr. Moon had a large collection of books. Lottie especially liked to read about people of other times and places.

Mrs. Moon also thought that it was important for children to learn the Bible. On Sundays the family attended the Baptist church in Scottsville, Virginia. The

Moons had helped to start this church.

Sunday was a day of rest in the Moon home. All work and play came to a stop. The family came home from church to a cold lunch because no cooking was allowed on Sunday. They spent the remainder of the day resting, reading, and visiting.

One Sunday, Lottie stayed home from church and cooked a hot meal for the family. Her parents were not pleased with her. After that they locked the kitchen when they went to church.

Even though Lottie often got into mischief, no one could stay angry with her for long. Her charm and sense of humor made people quickly forget how frequently she broke the rules.

The Moon home, like most homes of that time, had strict rules. However, Mr. and Mrs. Moon encouraged their children to think and to dream of the future.

Mrs. Moon often read to her children from the Bible and from life stories of important people. She read to them the story of Ann Judson, the first female Baptist foreign missionary from the United States. Lottie's eyes grew wide when her mother read about the dangers and strange experiences that Mrs. Judson and her husband faced in faraway Burma. Lottie wondered what it would be like to go so far away to live. It sounded exciting, but it also sounded sort of scary. She wondered why the Judsons had left their friends and family to go to Burma, and if they were glad they had gone.

2

Off to School

Lottie hugged her mother and ran to board the waiting stagecoach. A hundred different thoughts raced through Lottie's mind. She was 13 years old and she was about to begin the first big adventure of her life. The stagecoach she was boarding would take her to the Virginia Female Seminary near Roanoke, Virginia. There she would attend high school with approximately 100 other girls. She wondered what these girls would be like and where they would be from. She wondered if they would like to do the same things for fun that she did.

As Lottie waved to her mother from the window, she wished that her father could have been there to see her off also. However, Mr. Moon had died about a year ago. He had left instructions with his wife that some of his money was to be used to provide an education for all of his children.

Providing an education for girls was unusual for that time. Many families sent only their sons to high school.

Daughters stayed at home and learned from their mothers how to run a large household. Girls from well-to-do families usually married wealthy young men and had large homes. They devoted their time to overseeing the cooking, sewing, care of their children, and entertainment of guests.

Lottie's mother wanted her daughters to have good homes. But she allowed them freedom to choose what they wanted to do with their lives. About the same time that Lottie went away to high school, her older sister Orianna went to the Female Medical College of Pennsylvania to study to be a doctor. She became one of the first women doctors in the South.

As the stagecoach moved slowly toward Roanoke on that autumn day in 1854, Lottie carefully took in every sight and sound. This was her first step into the world on her own. She wanted to make the most of it.

At school Lottie made several new friends right away. Her cousin, Cary Ann Coleman, became her roommate.

Lottie believed in combining a lot of fun with her studies. Her keen sense of humor made her popular, but sometimes it got her into trouble.

At dawn April Fool's Day, Cary heard Lottie sneak out of the room. Cary knew that her roommate was up to something.

When Lottie returned, Cary sat straight up in bed. "Where have you been and what have you done?" she asked.

"Can't tell," Lottie replied. "You'll know later."

Cary fell back asleep. When she finally awoke, she jumped up and looked out the window.

"Lottie, why is the sun so bright? We must have overslept!" she exclaimed.

Lottie rolled over, laughing. "Of course we overslept," Lottie replied. "Everyone overslept. The bell didn't ring! Today is April Fool's Day!" The bell had not rung because Lottie had stuffed it with sheets and blankets early that morning. The news of Lottie's prank spread as classes began late that morning. The other

students looked up to this bright, fun-loving girl who brought excitement to their daily routine.

Lottie did not spend all of her time playing. She studied hard, and she did good work in her classes. She earned her best grades in French and Latin. Her mother was very happy to get reports of Lottie's good grades. She was not happy to read that Lottie was often absent from chapel services. She worried because Lottie showed no interest in church.

When Lottie was 16, she graduated from high school with a diploma in French. The name of the school had been changed to Hollins Institute. One of the essays that was read during the graduation ceremony was on the topic "Women's Rights." This topic was beginning to receive a lot of attention at that time. People were beginning to ask what roles women should fill outside of the home.

Lottie probably listened carefully to this essay. At 16 years of age, she had the beginning of a very good education. She must have wondered how she would use it and what she would do with her life.

3

A New Lottie

After graduating from Hollins, Lottie went back to Viewmont. She helped her mother run the farm and she taught her younger sister Edmonia. Lottie stayed at Viewmont for about a year.

She was busy, but she was restless. She wanted to get more education, but the University of Virginia in nearby Charlottesville was only open to men.

About this time some Baptist leaders in Virginia decided that women should be able to receive the same education that men received at the University. The leaders started the Albemarle Female Institute in Charlottesville. Women could study the same subjects at the Institute that men studied at the University of Virginia. This was a new day for women's education!

Lottie enrolled in classes at the new Albemarle Female Institute. She was excited at the chance to take university classes in Latin and Greek. She soon earned a reputation as a brilliant scholar. Her sharp mind and her love for fun again made her popular.

Lottie often teased new students by telling them that Professor Hart, the principal of the school, expected everyone to join the Baptist church the first Sunday they were there.

Lottie often boasted about her own lack of concern for religion. Once, another student asked her what the initial *D* in her name stood for. Lottie laughed and replied "Devil." She made fun of church and boasted that she had no need of it.

Lottie's Christian friends worried about her. But she was so brilliant that they were often afraid to try to talk to her about becoming a Christian. During Lottie's second year at the school, John Broadus held a revival in Charlottesville. Some of Lottie's Christian friends had early morning prayer meetings for the revival. Every day they prayed that Lottie would become a Christian.

Lottie heard that her friends were praying for her. She did not think that she needed to become a Christian. She decided to go to the revival just to make fun of it.

Something wonderful happened to Lottie during the revival service, however. Lottie had heard about Jesus since she was a little girl, but that night she really understood what Jesus had done for her. She could no longer ignore the fact that He had given His life to be her Saviour.

Lottie slipped quietly away from the meeting and went to her room. She prayed all night long. By morning she had settled the most important question of her life.

Imagine the other girls' surprise when Lottie appeared at their prayer meeting the next morning. She had not come to laugh at them. She had come to tell them that she had accepted Jesus as her Saviour.

It did not take long for people to see that Lottie's life was changed. She no longer made fun of Christians. She went to church every Sunday, and soon she was leading a student prayer meeting.

Often in church Lottie heard the preacher challenge the young people to give their lives to Christian work. He challenged the young men to go to other countries

as missionaries. As Lottie listened, she thought about her own life. She knew that women only went to the missions field as missionary wives. She wondered if this would always be true. She believed that there was work she could do as a missionary even if she were not married.

Lottie studied Greek, Latin, Italian, French, Spanish, and Hebrew. She did very good work. Her professors said that she was the best student they had ever taught. She was one of the first five women to receive a master of arts degree from the school. These five were the first women in the entire South to achieve this honor.

4

Lottie the Teacher

Lottie sat on the porch and watched the sun set over the hillside at Viewmont. The scene appeared peaceful, but Lottie knew it might not be peaceful much longer. The Civil War had come to Virginia. Northern and Southern soldiers were fighting each other in the nearby towns of Manassas and Bull Run. Many of the wounded soldiers were brought to Charlottesville to be cared for. Lottie's sister Orianna, now a doctor, treated many of them. Sometimes Lottie went to Charlottesville to help her. Most of the time Lottie helped her mother with the farm. Once again Lottie became the teacher for Edmonia. The war had prevented Eddie, as she was known, from going away to high school as Lottie had done.

Near the end of the war a messenger brought frightening news to Viewmont.

"The Yankees are coming! They're raiding farms and taking everything valuable." Lottie and her family hastily loaded food and clothing onto a wagon. Mrs.

Moon sent a servant to take the wagon far into the woods to protect it from the raiders. She gave Lottie the family jewels and silver and sent her to the apple orchard to bury them.

The raiders never appeared. Soon the household was back to normal, except for one thing. Lottie could not find the spots where she had buried the family treasures! Most of them were never found.

Finally, the war ended. The income from the family farm had greatly decreased during the war. Lottie needed to earn a living. She moved to Kentucky to teach in the Danville Female Academy. She also taught Sunday School and helped with other activities at the First Baptist Church.

Her interest in missions grew. She met two missionaries who had served in China. Lottie listened intently as they talked about life in China and the need for missionaries there. Perhaps China was where she should serve the Lord. She thought back to her childhood when her mother had read to her about brave Ann Judson. Mrs. Judson had served and died in faraway Burma.

Lottie felt this kind of bravery beginning to grow inside of her. The more she heard about China, the more she wanted to go there to share the gospel.

The time was not yet right, however. Southern Baptists were not yet willing to appoint single women as missionaries.

Lottie continued her work as a teacher. But she did not forget her dream of going to China. In the spring of 1870, her third year in Kentucky, Lottie was called home to Viewmont. Her mother was dying. After her mother died, Lottie stayed at Viewmont for the rest of the summer. She had long talks with Edmonia. She discovered that Edmonia also wanted to go to China as a missionary.

The next year Lottie had a wonderful opportunity. The town leaders of Cartersville, Georgia, decided to open a school for girls. They asked Lottie and a friend of hers, Anna Safford, to come to Cartersville to direct the school.

Lottie and Anna threw themselves wholeheartedly into their work at the new school. They used their own money to buy books and supplies. They did all they could to make the old building attractive. They even bought a piano and an organ.

Soon Cartersville Female High School was ready to open. On the first day 7 girls enrolled. Soon more than 100 students were attending the school.

Lottie joined the Cartersville Baptist Church. In addition to her work at the school, she taught Sunday School. She also spent many hours helping poor families in the community.

Lottie's friend, Anna Safford, helped at the Presbyterian church while Lottie was busy at the Baptist church. Both ladies were well liked by their students and by the people of the town. Everyone was happy when they agreed to stay another year.

Lottie's dreams of China were suddenly revived when she got the news that Edmonia was to be appointed as a missionary to that country. She would sail for China right away. Lottie could hardly believe it! How had the Foreign Mission Board agreed to appoint Edmonia, who was a single woman? Why had they changed their minds?

Edmonia had been writing letters to Mrs. Martha Crawford. Mrs. Crawford and her husband were missionaries in China. Mrs. Crawford was happy to hear that Edmonia wanted to come to China as a missionary. She told Edmonia that there was a lot of work that a single woman could do in China. She could visit Chinese women in their homes and tell them about Jesus. Chinese women almost never came to church with the men until a woman had led them to accept Jesus as Saviour.

The Crawfords offered to let Edmonia live in their home if she would come to China. This would be much safer for a single woman than living alone.

Edmonia wrote to the Foreign Mission Board requesting to go to China. The new director of the Foreign Mission Board took her request seriously. He knew that a single woman like Edmonia would have more time for house-to-house visiting than the missionary wives.

Women in Southern Baptist churches were beginning to organize in order to support missionaries. The women of five churches in Richmond, Virginia, agreed to pay Edmonia's salary, which would be $400 a year.

After a long trip by train across the United States and an even longer voyage by ship across the Pacific Ocean, Edmonia arrived in China. Almost at once she began to write to Lottie about the need for more missionaries. Her letters made Lottie want to go to China more than ever.

Edmonia also told Mr. and Mrs. Crawford about her talented sister. They wrote to the Foreign Mission Board asking that Lottie also be sent to China.

One Sunday, the pastor of Lottie's church preached on the need for more foreign missionaries. He used this verse for his sermon:

The harvest truly is
plenteous, but the labourers are few;
   Pray ye therefore the Lord
of the harvest that He will
   send forth labourers
into his harvest
   (Matthew 9:37-38 KJV).

Lottie understood that she could be a laborer in China, and that the harvest was all of the Chinese men, women, and children who needed to know Jesus.

At the end of the service, Lottie slipped quietly from the church. Once again she had a very important decision to make. After spending all afternoon in her room in prayer, she knew what she would do.

Lottie wrote to the Foreign Mission Board at once,

requesting to be sent to China. Her request was granted. As soon as the school year ended in Cartersville in 1873, Lottie was appointed as a missionary.

Lottie's students and their parents were sad to see her go.

Some of the people in Cartersville did not understand why she would leave their school to go to faraway China. However, her decision to go to China helped Baptist churches in Georgia to become more interested in missions. The women of several churches worked together to furnish her salary.

After visits with friends and family, Lottie boarded the train that would take her on the first part of her long journey to Tengchow,[1] China. At last she would join her sister in the work of which she had dreamed for so long.

[1]Tengchow is now named Penglai.

5

China at Last

The train trip across the United States was long and tiring. At last Lottie boarded the ship *Costa Rica* in the San Francisco harbor. She was ready to sail to China!

Lottie looked out over the Pacific Ocean. Her excitement was mixed with some sadness. She did not know if she would ever return to Virginia or see her family again.

She looked around at other missionaries traveling on the same ship. Several of them had long, sad faces. Are they thinking the same thoughts, Lottie wondered.

Lottie decided that she would not wear a sad face. She would not think about what she was leaving. She would look forward to where she was going. Edmonia had written to her about China, and she could hardly wait to get there. In the meantime, she would enjoy all of the wonderful things that she saw on her trip.

Lottie did enjoy the trip, except at mealtimes. Many times she was too seasick to eat.

Twenty-five days after leaving San Francisco, the ship

docked in Japan. It stopped in three Japanese cities before going on to China. The beautiful sights in these cities thrilled Lottie. She could not speak Japanese, but she managed to do a lot of sightseeing during the brief stops.

Between Japan and China, a storm almost wrecked the ship. The captain had to turn the ship around and go back to Japan. They sailed for China again a few days later.

At last the ship reached Shanghai, China. Mr. and Mrs. Crawford were there to meet Lottie. She was very glad to see them. Even more, she wanted to hurry to Tengchow to see Edmonia.

When Lottie finally arrived in Tengchow, she and Edmonia had a joyful reunion. Mr. Crawford had built an addition to his house to make room for Lottie. Edmonia helped her settle in. The two sisters talked for hours to catch up on news of family and friends.

Edmonia took Lottie to see the city. She wanted her to meet the Chinese people and to begin hearing the language. Everywhere they went, children ran up to touch them. The children asked Edmonia and Lottie all kinds of questions about themselves.

"What is your name?"

"How old are you?"

"Are you married?"

All of the children wanted to see Lottie because she was about the same size as they were. She was only four feet three inches tall. The other Americans they had seen were much taller.

Lottie thought the children were beautiful. They had shining black eyes and long pigtails. She did not even mind their endless questions. The hard thing for Lottie was that someone had to explain to her in English what the children said in Chinese.

The Chinese language was hard to learn. A Chinese teacher taught Lottie to speak and write it. She studied hard and she learned quickly. Lottie also learned all she could about Chinese life and history. She admired the

Chinese people. She especially admired the Chinese Christians who had enough courage to follow Jesus publicly. Most of their friends and family members were not Christians.

Some Chinese customs were hard for Lottie to accept. Wealthy Chinese families bound the feet of their little girls. Tight bandages kept their feet from growing. Deformed feet made it very hard for them to walk when they grew up.

Well-to-do Chinese women in the cities did not go to public places. They would not come to church with men. The only way that they would ever hear the gospel was for Christian women to visit them in their homes to tell them about Jesus. So this is what the women missionaries tried to do.

Often Chinese women in the cities would not let the missionaries come into their homes. Sometimes the missionaries were called "foreign devils" as they traveled through the streets.

The women missionaries found that they were welcomed in the small villages outside the city. In these villages women were more free to leave their homes. They were eager to see and hear the missionaries. Many of these village people had never seen a foreigner.

On Lottie's first trip to the villages, she was amazed at the response of the people. In every village people crowded around to listen as missionaries told about Jesus. The missionaries almost could not stop to eat lunch.

At the end of the day, Lottie thought about the many people who had heard the gospel. Then she thought about the hundreds of villages which they had not yet visited. She thought about the many Chinese who had not heard the gospel that day. She knew she had found the work that she loved best.

Lottie still could not forget the Chinese women and children in the city. Since the city women seldom left their homes, she knew she had to find ways to get them to invite her into their homes. This was not easy, but

Lottie did not give up. Slowly she was able to win the friendship of some of the children. They took her into their homes, and she was able to tell their mothers about Jesus. Every time Lottie entered another Chinese home, she thanked God for this special opportunity to share the gospel.

6

Goodbye to Edmonia

A knock at the door woke Lottie from her brief after-noon nap. She opened the door to find Mrs. Crawford standing in the doorway.

"I know this is the New Year holiday," began Mrs. Crawford, "but Mrs. Lan needs our help!"

Mrs. Crawford went on to explain. Mrs. Lan was a Christian Chinese lady whose children came to the mis-sionaries' schools. During the holiday she had gone to her family's village. She had told the people about Jesus. Many of them had come to her to learn more. Now she had sent someone to ask the missionaries to come and help her teach them.

Lottie, Edmonia, and the other women missionaries left at once on the eight-mile trip to Mrs. Lan's village. When the other missionaries had to come back to the city, Lottie and Edmonia stayed in the village. On Sun-day they had the first worship service ever held in that village.

Lottie and Edmonia were happy as they started back

to Tengchow the next day. As they traveled, the weather turned cold and windy. Edmonia became sick. Many weeks went by but she did not get better. Instead, she became weaker. It was hard for her to work.

One of Edmonia's favorite parts of her work was the school that she ran for little boys. As Edmonia became weaker, Lottie helped her more with the school.

The two sisters had a dream of opening a school for girls. Most Chinese families believed girls did not need to go to school. They kept their daughters at home until the daughters married and left to live with their husbands.

Lottie knew that their dream of a school for girls would require a lot of work. Missionaries would have to visit in Chinese homes many times. They would have to convince the parents that their daughters should go to school. Lottie and Edmonia could not do this work alone.

Lottie often wrote letters to the Foreign Mission Board. She asked them to send two women missionaries to help her and Edmonia. She wrote about their work in the city and in the villages. She wrote about the many Chinese people who were not hearing the gospel because there were not enough missionaries to tell them.

The secretary of the Foreign Mission Board sent copies of Lottie's letters to women's missionary societies in Baptist churches. These women met together to pray for Lottie and the other missionaries. They also gave money to help the missionaries in their work. Women's missionary societies in Virginia and Georgia raised money so that one day Lottie and Edmonia could have a house of their own in China. At this time they still lived with Mr. and Mrs. Crawford.

Lottie worked hard to run Edmonia's school. She kept hoping that Edmonia would soon be well enough to work again. At the same time that Lottie was directing the school, she continued to make trips to the villages to share the gospel. Often she was tired, but she loved her work. Lottie became excited when women and children in the villages believed in Jesus. She almost forgot how tired she was.

Lottie had one problem that she could not forget, however. Edmonia was not getting better. Instead, she was getting worse. The missionaries decided that Edmonia needed to go back to the United States. They hoped that a long rest and the better climate in Virginia would help her get well.

Edmonia was too sick to travel alone. Lottie made the long trip to Virginia with her. They reached Viewmont on December 22, 1876, just in time for Christmas. While Edmonia rested, Lottie visited with her brothers and sisters. She was very glad to see everyone again.

Lottie wanted to return to China right away, but this was not possible. The Foreign Mission Board did not have any money to pay her way. While she was waiting to return to China, Lottie visited women's missionary societies. She told them about her work and she encouraged them to keep giving money to missions.

The women in the missionary societies wanted Lottie to be able to return to China. They thought about the money they had raised to build a house for Lottie and Edmonia. The money was still in the bank. The women decided to use this money to pay for Lottie's trip back to China. They also promised to send money for her living expenses.

At last Lottie was able to sail to China again. This time she was not going to some faraway land where everything was strange to her. This time she was going back to people she had grown to love. This time she was going home.

7

A School for Girls

Lottie opened the door of the schoolroom quietly. She stopped for a moment before entering. The 13 girls present were reciting the lessons they had memorized. Each spoke aloud at the same time. This made the schoolroom a very noisy place.

Lottie listened to the girls. She remembered Edmonia's dream of opening a girl's school in Tengchow. Lottie had taken up that dream. She had worked hard to start the school. She wanted the Chinese girls to learn to read. She also wanted them to study the Bible and become Christians.

The hardest part of opening the school was getting the girls to come. The wealthy people would not let their daughters attend school. Some poor families allowed their daughters to come because the school provided free food, medical care, and a place to live. The parents had only to provide their daughters' clothes.

When the school opened, Lottie had only 5 students. Soon this number grew to 13. She taught the girls reading, arithmetic, and geography. She used a book of Bible stories to teach reading. She also gave the girls singing lessons.

The class was small, but the girls worked hard. They performed good memory work. Some of them memorized the entire book of Matthew or Mark from the New Testament.

A few of the girls became Christians. This was not an easy thing for them to do. Often a girl's parents would not let her become a Christian.

The school grew slowly. It became harder to find enough money to feed the girls and run the school. Lottie wrote to some of the women's missionary societies in the United States for help. Several of these societies agreed to send the Foreign Mission Board $15 a year to pay the way for one student at the school. Lottie wrote to each society to tell the ladies how their student was doing in school.

Lottie wrote many letters to the missionary societies. She always asked them to pray for her and for the other missionaries. She asked them to write to her. Getting letters from home helped the missionaries when they were lonely. They needed to know that the people at home believed in their work.

The missionaries were often lonely and tired. There were only a few missionaries in North China, and they were working to share the gospel with many, many people. They often worked too much and did not get enough rest. Sometimes their health suffered from overwork, the harsh climate, and exposure to a variety of diseases.

Lottie saw what was happening to these overworked missionaries. Some of them, like Edmonia, became so ill that they had to leave China forever.

Lottie believed that this could be prevented. She thought all missionaries needed a chance to get away from their work for a time of rest. She believed they would come back to their work stronger and able to do a better job.

Lottie wrote a bold letter to the Foreign Mission Board. She suggested that each missionary come to the United States for a time of rest after he had worked for ten years. This time at home would be called a furlough.

This was a new idea! Furloughs were not begun right away, but they were begun later. Today, all missionaries who serve in other countries can come back to the United States for furloughs. They can be thankful for Lottie Moon who suggested the idea a long time ago!

Lottie also knew that it was hard for a missionary to leave for furlough when there was no one to do his work. She knew that the small group of missionaries could not possibly share the gospel with everyone in North China. She did not understand why more missionaries did not come to help them. Often she wrote to the Foreign Mission Board. She begged them to send more missionaries to China.

In the meantime, Lottie found several ways to fight her own loneliness and exhaustion. She read a lot of books. She often took walks down to the sea. Sometimes she went swimming. In her yard she raised flowers.

In the evening as she worked in her flower garden, she thought of the flowers on the hillsides back in Virginia. She whispered a prayer:

"Dear God, please help the Christians back in the United States to care about the people of China. Please send more of them to help us share your gospel with the Chinese people. Amen."

8

The Cookie Lady

Lottie awoke early and began her morning chores with excitement. The house must look perfect! A new missionary, Miss Mattie Roberts, would arrive today! Lottie could hardly believe it. She had waited so long for someone to help share the gospel with the Chinese women. Today the new missionary would finally be here!

When Mattie arrived, Lottie became her teacher. She introduced Mattie to Chinese customs and helped her adjust to life in China. Lottie shared with Mattie what she had learned from her years as a missionary.

Mattie listened to Lottie carefully. She wanted to learn all she could. As Lottie watched Mattie, Lottie became excited about the future. It was wonderful to see a young missionary who was so eager to begin work.

Soon more new missionaries came. Lottie greeted them joyfully and helped them choose the places where they would work. There was plenty of work for everyone.

Lottie was now giving all of her time to visiting in Tengchow and the villages nearby. She had realized that she was not able to operate the girls' school and keep up with the long hours of visiting. She had decided that visiting to share the gospel was the most important work for her. With sorrow, she closed the school. She hoped that someday it would open again.

The new missionaries had dreams of carrying the gospel farther and farther into China. Three of them traveled 120 miles to the city of P'ingtu. They came back telling about crowds of people who had followed them, wanting to hear the gospel.

Lottie went to P'ingtu to see for herself. It took four days to get there. She spent the nights in rough country inns which were not comfortable or clean.

When Lottie arrived in P'ingtu, she was amazed. Everywhere she went, there were people ready to listen to the gospel. The people of P'ingtu had seen few foreigners because their city was so far away from a seaport. Many of them wanted to hear all they could about God.

Lottie stayed in P'ingtu for a month. She told many people about Jesus during that time. She thought about what it would be like to live in P'ingtu and work as a missionary.

Soon Lottie decided she must move to P'ingtu. Someone must live there to tell the gospel to these people who were so eager to hear it. Lottie felt that she was the one to work in P'ingtu.

There were now other missionaries in Tengchow to carry on Lottie's work there. A missionary working in P'ingtu would be separated by many miles from other Americans. Lottie felt that she could do this more easily than the younger missionaries could. She understood the Chinese customs better than they did. She had learned to eat Chinese food. She knew how to deal with loneliness.

Lottie returned to Tengchow to get her belongings. She gathered together warm clothing, medicines, food, books, a mattress, bed covering, and a cookstove. She had these things loaded onto mules for the long trip.

Mr. Chao and his wife were Chinese members of the Baptist church in Tengchow. They went with Lottie to P'ingtu to help her take care of her house.

Lottie's house in P'ingtu was very simple. It had a dirt floor and thatched roof. It was heated by a fire in one room. Lottie received guests in this room during the day. At night she slept here because it was the warmest room in the house.

Lottie knew that many of the people in P'ingtu did not trust foreigners. She was sometimes called "devil woman" or "foreign devil," as she had been in Tengchow. Lottie tried to be a good friend and neighbor so the people would trust her. She wanted them to believe the gospel and accept Jesus as their Saviour.

Lottie made cookies and offered them to the children she met. At first, the children would not eat the cookies. People had told them cookies made by the "foreign devil" would poison them.

Finally the children could not resist. They ate the cookies, which were delicious. They discovered that the cookies were not poison after all. They wanted Lottie to be their friend. The children took Lottie into their homes. Lottie was then able to tell their mothers about Jesus. The children began calling Lottie "the cookie lady" instead of "foreign devil."

Lottie made her cookies with the recipe below.

PLAIN TEA CAKE[1]

Three teacups of dry sugar, one of butter, one of sour milk, four pints of flour, 3 eggs, well beaten; half a teaspoonful of soda. Flavor to taste; roll thin, and bake in a quick oven.

[1]Claude Rhea, compiler, *Lottie Moon Cook Book* (Waco, Texas—London, England: Word Books, 1969), 183.

9

Alone in P'ingtu

Winter came to P'ingtu. Lottie began wearing heavy Chinese clothes over her American clothes to stay warm. She discovered that when she wore Chinese clothes, people on the street were more friendly to her. She began wearing her hair in a Chinese style, too. She almost looked like a Chinese person. This made it easier for Chinese people to accept her.

Lottie was soon well accepted in and around P'ingtu. Within a few months she made 122 visits to nearby villages. Everywhere she went, she shared the gospel. Soon she had more invitations to visit than she could accept.

In P'ingtu Lottie faced a special problem. In her work in Tengchow, she had usually taught only women and children. One of the men missionaries or a Chinese pastor taught the men. According to Chinese and American customs, women did not teach men. In P'ingtu there were no men missionaries and few Chinese men who had been Christians very long.

The Chinese men wanted to learn about Jesus. If Lottie did not teach them, they would not be taught.

Lottie decided that she must teach the men as well as the women and children. She could not refuse when they wanted to hear the gospel. Often, when she was teaching women and children in a house, groups of men stood outside every window to listen.

Lottie loved her work in P'ingtu, but she knew that she must rest too. She needed to visit the other missionaries and hear English spoken again. In P'ingtu she heard only Chinese.

In June, when the weather became very hot in P'ingtu, Lottie went to Tengchow for a visit. She went back to her house, which was at the Little Cross Roads. During the summer she visited with the other missionaries in Tengchow. She shared their joys and sorrows. She tried to help them whenever she could.

Soon Lottie felt refreshed and ready to return to P'ingtu. However, some of the missionaries were very sick. Lottie impatiently remained several extra months to help with their work.

At last, Lottie was able to leave for P'ingtu. She made the 120-mile trip in a mule cart. The people of P'ingtu welcomed her back. She was glad to see them, too. She was happy to get back to her work there.

Lottie worked hard, but there was too much work in P'ingtu for one person to do. Lottie needed more missionaries to help her. She also needed a furlough. She had not visited the United States in ten years. She wanted to visit her sister Edmonia and walk over the hillsides of Virginia. She wanted to go to the Baptist churches and tell the people there about her work in China. She wanted them to know about the need for missionaries in China.

Lottie wanted very much to go to the United States. But she did not want to leave P'ingtu until there was someone to do her work. She could not leave when there was no one else to teach the people of P'ingtu about Christ.

Lottie began to write letters again. She wrote to the Foreign Mission Board. She told them that she needed a furlough. She asked them to send more missionaries to China.

Lottie also wrote to the women's missionary societies. She asked them to pray that God would call people to go to China as missionaries. She also encouraged them to give more money to missions.

Often Lottie's letters were printed in Baptist newspapers in the United States. Everyone who read these newspapers learned about the need for more missionaries in China. In one of her letters, Lottie suggested two ideas. One was that women organize the Woman's Missionary Union to support missionaries with prayer and money. The other idea was that women in Baptist churches set aside the week before Christmas to pray for missions and to give money to missions. Christmas is a celebration of Jesus' birth. Lottie thought that the best way to celebrate Christmas would be to pray and give money for Jesus' work on earth.

Lottie continued her work in P'ingtu. Often she was tired, but she found it hard to say no to anyone who asked her to teach them.

One day Lottie came in from her work very tired. She had visited in homes all afternooon. She had taught reading to Chinese girls all morning.

As she sat down to enjoy a few moments rest, Lottie heard a knock at the door. She was surprised to find three men standing there.

"Please, Miss Moon," they said politely. "Please come to our village to teach us about Jesus. Our friend, Mr. Dan, heard of Jesus when he was traveling in another city. He wants you to teach all of us about Jesus. You can stay in Mr. Dan's home while you are in our village."

The three men were from the village of Sha-ling, about ten miles away. There was no Christian church in Sha-ling. They had walked all the way to P'ingtu to ask for Lottie's help.

How could Lottie say no? She left for Sha-ling as soon as she could. There she taught the people Bible verses, hymns, and simple prayers.

Often she taught for 14 hours a day. Once again she broke Chinese and American customs by teaching men as well as women. She could not turn away anyone who came to her to hear the gospel.

And still Lottie prayed that more missionaries, both men and women, would come to China soon.

10

Lottie Gets a Rest

Every day Lottie waited eagerly for the Chinese mail carrier to come. Letters from friends and family members always made her feel better. She always hoped for a special letter from the Foreign Mission Board announcing that a new missionary was coming to help her.

Lottie had a reason to expect this special letter. As she had hoped, the women and children of the Southern Baptist Convention had organized Woman's Missionary Union. At Christmas, they had taken their first Christmas offering for foreign missions. They had set a goal of $2,000. The money would be used to send two new missionaries to China. She could hardly wait to hear the results.

At last the letter came. Lottie ripped it open and began to read. She could hardly believe her eyes. The offering collected was more than $3,000! This was enough money to send three new women missionaries to China.

Soon Miss Fannie Knight came to P'ingtu to work

with Lottie. Lottie helped Fannie learn Chinese customs. She learned quickly. She worked hard and was a great help to Lottie. The other two new women missionaries worked in Tengchow.

Lottie was happy to have Fannie to help her. Many Chinese were becoming Christians, and Fannie helped teach them.

Fannie and Lottie both taught the men and the women. They also led the worship services.

The church needed a missionary pastor. Lottie and Fannie prayed that a missionary couple would come to P'ingtu. Lottie wrote letters to Baptist pastors asking them to consider coming to China as missionaries.

The next year, their prayer was answered. Mr. and Mrs. T. J. League came to P'ingtu as missionaries. Now Lottie could make plans for the furlough she needed so much. It had been 14 years since she had been to Virginia or seen any of her family. She wanted to see them very much. She also wanted to tell the Baptists in the United States about the work in China. She wanted to speak to them in person and tell them how they could help.

Soon Lottie sailed to America. She could hardly wait to get to Edmonia's little house in Scottsville, Virginia. She was ready for a rest!

As soon as Lottie reached Scottsville in 1891, she began receiving invitations to speak to women's missionary societies. The women wanted to hear about her work in China.

Lottie wanted to tell the women all about her work, but that would have to wait. Lottie was completely exhausted by the years of too much work and too little rest. She knew she needed a long rest now so her body could recover. This was the only way she would ever be able to return to China.

For six months Lottie stayed with Edmonia. She took long walks, visited with relatives, and ate healthy foods. Soon she began to get her strength back.

In the spring Lottie felt much better. She began vis-

iting missionary societies in churches, telling them about her work in China. She traveled south to Cartersville, Georgia, where she had taught school. Her students were now adults. They were excited to see her again.

Lottie also attended the meeting of Woman's Missionary Union in Atlanta, Georgia. Women from all over the Southern Baptist Convention were there. She told them of the great need for more missionaries. She told them about the many Chinese in P'ingtu who were eager to hear the gospel. She left them with this question, "What will you do for China?"

Lottie spoke to women's missionary societies in many more churches. Each time, she asked the women to pray that more missionaries would come to China. She also asked them to give money to missions. The women listened, and they responded. They knew that Lottie had given her whole life to missions in China. Her example led them to want to help.

Children also wanted to help. Many children in Virginia had hens which they called missionary hens. They named their hens after missionaries. Some named their hens after Lottie Moon. The children sold the eggs from the hens and gave the money to missions.

Lottie enjoyed telling about her work. She was pleased when her listeners wanted to help with missions. She was also eager to return to China. She knew that there was much work for her to do there.

On November 21, 1893, Lottie sailed to China again. More than ever, she felt like she was going home. Her furlough had refreshed her. It had given her new strength for the work that she loved so much.

11

The Little Cross Roads

Lottie was both happy and sad to arrive back in China. She was happy to get back to her work, and she was happy to see the Chinese Christians and the missionaries with whom she worked.

However, she was saddened to learn some of the missionaries had left the mission. These missionaries did not like the way the Foreign Mission Board operated the mission. They disagreed with the leaders of the Foreign Mission Board about many things. One of the things these missionaries disagreed with was the use of mission money to pay Chinese pastors. They thought that the Chinese churches should pay their own pastors. These missionaries started their own mission so they could make their own decisions and work in the way they wanted.

Lottie wished that the missionaries could have worked out their differences. She wished that they could all have stayed together. The mission needed more missionaries, not fewer. Some of the missionaries

who left had been in China many years. Lottie was sorry to see them go. She remained loyal to the Foreign Mission Board, however.

In spite of these problems, there was much work to do. When the remaining missionaries met to plan their work, they looked to Lottie as their leader. She had served in China longer than any of them. She helped them make important decisions about the future of their work.

Lottie knew that the Chinese people in P'ingtu were still eager to hear the gospel. She thought it would be better for younger missionaries to go to P'ingtu to work. She would work in Tengchow and the villages nearby. The people in Tengchow were not as eager to hear the gospel as those in P'ingtu. However, many of them respected Lottie because of her many years of work in China. She was also accepted more easily because she dressed in Chinese clothes and respected their laws.

Lottie settled into her house at the Little Cross Roads in Tengchow. She began at once to visit in and around the city. Everywhere she went, people gathered around to ask her questions. She turned these questions into opportunities to teach the people. She gave them Bible pictures and simple books and tracts.

Lottie tried to share the gospel with as many Chinese people as possible. In three months she visited 84 villages. At night she returned to her house at the Little Cross Roads. She was thankful for her quiet, peaceful home where she could rest.

China and Japan went to war against each other. Some of the Chinese people thought that the missionaries might be Japanese spies. However, the Chinese officials in Tengchow asked the missionaries to stay. They thought that the presence of the American missionaries would help to protect the city from the Japanese.

Lottie went to P'ingtu for a visit at Christmas. On her way home, she learned that the Japanese had attacked Tengchow. By the time she reached the city, the other

missionaries had fled on a United States warship.

Lottie was the only foreigner in the city! What would she do?

Immediately some of the Chinese leaders of Tengchow came to Lottie. They asked her to stay in the city to help keep the Chinese people calm.

Lottie agreed to stay. She believed that God would protect her until she had finished the work that He wanted her to do.

Soon the other missionaries were able to return. When the Tengchow Baptist Church opened again, crowds of Chinese people came. They appreciated Lottie's presence and encouragement in their time of danger. They wanted to hear what the missionaries were teaching. Many of these Chinese people became Christians. The Tengchow Baptist Church grew rapidly.

Lottie continued visiting in the villages. She enjoyed this work very much. She loved the outdoors, and the village people were very friendly.

The work in the villages was hard. The long hours of traveling and teaching left Lottie tired. Often she had throat trouble. Sometimes she was caught in heavy rains, which made traveling more difficult.

Lottie realized she needed times of rest between her travels. Sometimes she stayed at home at the Little Cross Roads and let people come to see her. Chinese friends came to visit or to ask for help with their problems. Lottie often taught lessons in her home. Missionary friends came for a rest when they were tired or ill. In Lottie's home they found good food, good conversation, and encouragement to continue their work.

Lottie noticed how tired the other missionaries were. She knew that too much work was ruining their health. She began writing letters to the Foreign Mission Board again. As always, she asked them to send more missionaries to China.

Lottie was also worried about her own health. She feared that she would not be able to travel to the villages much longer. She opened a day school for boys and girls. Having boys and girls in the same school was a new idea in China.

Lottie hired a teacher for the school. She worked with the teacher on Monday. On Tuesday through Saturday she visited the villages. Sunday was a busy day with Chinese and English worship services in the morning and Bible classes in the afternoon.

Lottie was getting older. It was not easy for her to keep up such a demanding schedule. Sometimes she had to stop all of her work and rest. This was the only way that she could recover and go on with her work.

Lottie knew that she could not work this hard forever. If the work was to continue, she must have someone to help her soon. Again, Lottie took up her pen to ask Southern Baptists in the United States to send more missionaries.

In the meantime, Lottie determined to do all she could to help the Chinese people hear the gospel.

12

Help Has Come

Lottie gazed at the dinner table in silent wonder. She could hardly believe her eyes when she saw the number of places set for the evening meal. Soon every chair would be filled, and Lottie would serve her guests a delicious dinner.

The missionary couple, Jesse and Rebecca Owen, was the first to come in to dinner. They were living in Lottie's guestrooms to be near their work in Tengchow. Soon the new missionaries, Mary Willeford and Jessie Pettigrew, arrived. Lottie's house was almost like home to these two young women. They studied Chinese there, and they came to Lottie often for advice.

Jessie Pettigrew was the first trained missionary nurse to be sent to China by the Foreign Mission Board. Jessie had grown up hearing stories about Lottie Moon and her work. As she became an adult, Jessie felt God wanted her to go to China as a missionary. She met Lottie when Lottie was in the United States on furlough. Now Jessie was here to do the work she had heard Lottie tell about.

As the group gathered for dinner, Lottie thanked God for each person. All of her letters and prayers over the years had not been in vain. Southern Baptists were responding to her challenge. More missionaries were coming to China. They were coming because they had heard about China through Lottie's letters.

As the number of missionaries increased, Lottie decided that it was time for her to visit her family in the United States again. She did not want to leave her work, but her sister Edmonia and her brother Isaac had been very sick. Lottie wanted to see them very much. She also wanted to report on the progress of the work in China to the many Southern Baptist women in the United States who had given money and prayed to make the missions work possible.

Lottie visited Edmonia and Isaac upon arrrival in the United States. She also visited her cousins, nieces, and nephews. She enjoyed the beautiful Virginia countryside. She spoke to women in many churches about missions. Then she prepared to return to China.

Some of Lottie's friends and relatives tried to persuade her to retire and stay in Virginia. But Lottie knew she must return to China. China was her home. Her work there was the joy of her life. A young relative asked why Aunt Lottie had never married. Lottie did not say much in response. She only said that God had first claim on her life.

In February 1904, Lottie sailed to China again. When she reached Tengchow, she was pleased at what she saw. The missionaries had opened a new school to train Chinese pastors. A Baptist hospital was being built.

Lottie also found that the Chinese people were more eager than ever to have an education. She decided to expand her school to include anyone who wanted to learn. Soon she had schools for children, for older boys, and for older girls. Lottie enjoyed her schools very much. When a student became a Christian and was baptized, it gave her great joy.

Lottie also opened her home to women from the villages who came for her to teach them. They stayed in her guest rooms. Lottie used her own money to feed them. Often she had as many as 15 women and their children staying with her.

Lottie also helped to train new missionaries. She greeted them warmly when they arrived and invited them to spend their first weeks in her home. There they enjoyed good meals and lively conversation. Lottie's friendship helped them with their homesickness.

Lottie also helped the new missionaries learn Chinese customs. She arranged for them to have a Chinese teacher to help them learn the language. She helped them select a Chinese name.

Lottie took the new women missionaries with her to the villages. She showed them how to be accepted by Chinese people. She taught them how to direct a conversation to tell someone about Christ. When she thought the new missionaries were ready, she let them work on their own.

Lottie's schools continued to grow. Some of the schools met in Lottie's house. There were always many children playing in her yard. Lottie loved the children and they loved her. She could be stern when they did not obey her, but she always made them feel loved and important.

The missionaries' children also loved Lottie. They liked to visit her home and listen to the exciting stories she told. They also liked the cookie jar which Lottie always kept full.

Sadness soon came to the mission. War broke out in China. At the same time, a bad disease called the plague began to spread. The plague killed many people. To add to the problem, many crops were destroyed by floods, and there was not much food. Some of the Chinese people had to eat sweet potato vines, roots, and leaves to stay alive.

Lottie wrote letters to Baptists in the United States begging for money to help feed the Chinese people. She also gave her own money to feed them. She took starving Chinese people into her home. Often she went without food so they could have something to eat. She helped care for those who were sick or injured in the war.

Lottie worried about the Chinese people. She felt helpless and sad as she watched so many of them suffer. She wanted so much to help them.

The other missionaries began to worry about Lottie. They did not know that she was not eating. Sometimes they sent their children to spend the day with her to cheer her up.

Lottie continued to give away her food. She would not eat while people around her were starving. Worry and lack of food soon left Lottie too weak to keep working. The other missionaries decided that she must go to the United States for a rest. Cynthia Miller, a missionary nurse, would go with Lottie to care for her.

Lottie hated to leave the Chinese people in this time of great need, but her health was so bad that there was no other choice.

Lottie was so weak that she slept for several days on the ship. When she awoke, she whispered to her nurse the words of the song, "Jesus Loves Me." A few days later, on Christmas Eve 1912, the ship was in the port of Kobe, Japan. It was here that Lottie Moon closed her eyes for the last time. She went to meet the Saviour whom she had served so faithfully.

Her Work Is Ours

Lottie Moon spent her entire life telling people in China about Jesus. Because of her example, many people have gone to countries around the world as missionaries.

In 1918 the Christmas offering that she had suggested was named the Lottie Moon Christmas Offering for Foreign Missions. This offering has increased greatly over the years. It now supplies about one-half of the money for Southern Baptist foreign missions work.

Lottie Moon would be very pleased to know that Southern Baptists observe the Week of Prayer for Foreign Missions each December. She would also be pleased to know that more than 3,700 missionaries are being supported by the Lottie Moon Christmas Offering and the Cooperative Program. She would be pleased to know that more than one million women, girls, and preschoolers are organized for missions through WMU.

This year, when you give to the Lottie Moon Christmas Offering, remember a brave little woman of long ago who taught Southern Baptists how important it is to share the gospel with people everywhere.

About the Writer

Ann Kilner Hughes is the director of alumni activities at Averett College in Danville, Virginia. A former editor at Woman's Missionary Union, SBC, she has also taught school. Ann first read about Lottie Moon as a member of Girl's Auxiliary (the forerunner to Girls in Action). She wrote this book so that children of today can also read the story of Lottie Moon, the great pioneer in missions.

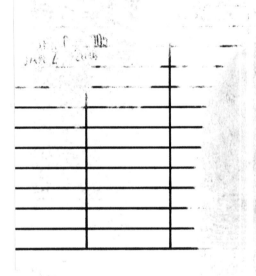